The Next True Story
Of My Life

Lois Holub

To Susie
with gratitude
for your love, support,
& faith! — Lois

RAIN CROW

PRESS

ISBN-13: 978-1502720238
ISBN-10: 150272023X

Cover art by Osa Hale
Book design by author and Donald Mitchell
Bio and cover photo by Alan Hale

For my daughters

Jamaica Beth
and
Osa Carmen

and for my sisters everywhere.

What would happen
if one woman told the truth about her life?
The world would split open.
-Muriel Rukeyser

Contents

The Mommy Poems

The Next True Story Of My Life

Haiku

The World Split Open

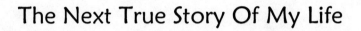
The Next True Story Of My Life

The Mommy Poems

Birth Spell

It started on the beach in broad daylight.
Your father went one way, into the rocks,
and I surrendered to the flat, southern stretch.
(My belly, you, did not like climbing.)
Walking, singing,
marching as if I could shake you down
I wandered toward the hill away from the shore.

Succulent, rubbery blooms color the dry sand,
fill the low air with pollen and bees.
There are other sounds, heard with the
surface of my skin.
I walk humming, while an owl's feather
leads me to the place

where there is a flat rim of iron (later I think of blood)
with an opening in the west.
As if I have always known how to do this,
I gather the stones for north and south,
east and center.
With my body encircling yours
I circle the wheel and pray.

I ask the tides for their movement
and the earth for her pull.
For guidance and strength
but mostly I say
"You must help me.
Bring this baby out."
When I can stand no longer I lie back in sand.
Daydreams appear,
guarded by the sun and a web of seasalt.

Evening waited. I could smell it
when your father and I met again,

turned together toward home.

And then evening broadened into night,
night into midnight,
and in the wolf's hour of darkness
a deep fire burst into being.
The spell was cast
and you began to speak aloud
in dance
and waves
and water song.

Wings

Witnessing our first ballet, my seven year-old
daughter and I
whisper through *The Magic Flute*,
eat M & Ms, hold hands, laugh and clap,
amazed.
On the way back to the car, afterwards,
amid the throng of our fellow ballet watchers,
we dance and leap and twirl up the night sidewalk.

Guess what I'm going to ask Santa for,
my daughter says the next day.
A pony? A bigger bike? Ballet shoes?
Nope, she answers.
Give me a hint, I tell her.
Well, she begins, it's something I don't know
if anybody's invented yet.
Oh. I think I give up. Tell me.
She looks at me and says *Wings*.

She wants to fly. She worked on wings last summer,
pulling tall grass up by the roots,
tying the stalks together with twine, adding
peacock feathers and flapping off the porch.
Now she will ask Santa.

My beautiful love, the power of your faith
is remarkable.
Not the faith that Santa—or anyone—can give you wings,
(I don't know if he can, you said to me, but he might *try,)*
but this: the faith in knowing you can dream, desire,
ask for the uninvented.
You were born with wings, my sweet,
whose brightness shadows the sun.

Photograph Albums

Framed, encased, your life coded and filed
by season, I put your pictures in scrapbooks.
They fill the shelf, full. Growing in number.
The camera clicks and whirs

catching more of you: Christmas, birthday
and the times when you thought no one was watching.
It's a need I have:
you keep changing.

You were two days old. New.
Strangers approached us at the laundromat.
"How tiny she is," they would say, "You forget the feet,
the fingers, how small they are," looking at your

face, smiling your smile—and I thought to
myself Not me! I will never forget you here
in my arms. And I saved you, a baby asleep in a blanket,

a baby surrounded by people who,
loving you, could finally love themselves.
The camera keeps what I finally could not. Now
there's too much. You have grown, leaping, out of my arms.

We look at your pictures together. Gathering up
a whole lifetime in laps full of color, I pretend
time has stopped ticking
and I have all of you, safe. That these photos

show not what is gone but what stays
undisturbed. There is something about this
you'll help me release. Complete
in yourself you slide off the sofa,
the baby in the books no longer of

interest as you put on your coat to go play
outside. In the trees. The fields. You
claim your world, and I know, with longing,
you may always come back but you cannot be kept.

Grief

My first memory of snow:
I am walking into the backyard
and I don't see anything that used to be there.
The swing set, the big bushes by the fence,
the ground has changed.
I move slowly, watching my boots to see if they change too.
My mother calls, "Look behind you!"
and I turn to see footprints,
dreadful green coming up through the white.
Something awful is following me.
Afraid, I start to cry.

There is a patchwork of old death marking the land
around our house.
One cat buried under the walnut tree,
another by the pasture gate.
A rabbit laid down beneath the flowering apple,
several birds in the garden.
Sixteen chickens in three mass graves
out back in the field.
Green comes growing out of these bones
bright as stained glass in the sun.

I have been unwillingly afraid of death
since childhood when my piano teacher fell over
during our recital and died.
By my mid-twenties I thought the fear had passed.
Then I had a daughter.
For the first two years of her life I was terrified
that she would die.
Then I was terrified that I would die and she would forget me.
Now there are times grief puts me on like a second skin
and I must move with its movements, dream its dreams
until it escapes again out my mouth,
my eyes, the palms of my hands.

I wish I had been raised by a tribe of people
who let death be,
who had a use for it.
I hold my daughter when it is her turn to cry
warm, bitter tears of sadness.
She can't tell me the words
and I understand this, too.
I want to go outside with her when spring comes,
press our bodies to the ground in the new sun
where we can smell it,
where, together, we can learn to hear the language
of transformation.

No Lullaby But This

Tonight sleep goes walking
hours before dawn without me.
The bed gets hot,
the baby pokes tender places inside.
I finally wander out to the sofa to wait for sleep's return,
that casual child who robs me of peace
until she returns safe and whole.

The stars are out.
I would like to know the sounds they make.
What I hear is a refrigerator fan,
water dripping,
a small clock's mechanical pulse inside a cabinet
across the room.
Walls that sigh.
I hear the grinding of small teeth,
ashes falling through the grate of the wood stove,
the soft beat of blood in my brain.
There is no silence,
no lullaby but this: the cotton tune of my breath
finding its way through the dark.

3:00 A.M. Ice Storm, Six Months Pregnant, Four Days Before War

On the outside
life falls dead to earth.
Everywhere are mountains with their trees cut away
and what is left moves down through the rivers
into our yards.
Encased in ice, the naked land weeps
when touched by warmth.
Farther on the outside,
so far it curves back to live in my house
is imminent war.
Imminent death.
Mothers with their children cut away,
the rest moving down through the desert into our TVs,
our gas tanks.
> I just woke up from a dream
> where my daughter and I had on gas masks
> but we breathed in the poison anyway,
> unknowing.
On the outside so much falls.
So much is unknown, then known wrong.

On the inside
the baby taps in water code to remind me,
this primal language for unspoken voice,
and I remember without words to tell.

Inside someone grows, turning in a private rhythm
of blood, of seeds underground.
Inside is something new and even further in,
so far it circles back to be my cells,
my soul,
is someone ancient
someone known
someone coming from the inside out.

I Always Sang To Your Sister

I always sang to your sister,
starting before she was born.
As my belly grew so did my repertoire.
She came into the world already familiar
with Amazing Grace and Danny Boy.
When she was three she could sing all the verses
of Old Man River and Swing Low Sweet Chariot.
I would hold her at night in the rocking chair
and the music would move from my mouth to her ears
as simply as breathing.

You did not get many songs from me in your saltwater sac.
Instead you heard the buzz of the alarm clock, typewriter keys
snapping in the darkness,
the tense voice of my ambivalent faith.
Your embryonic tongue knew the taste of my fears
as surely as I prayed you would also know my love.

Now it is our turn in the rocking chair.
I hold you with your head tucked under my chin
and breathe in the smell of you.
The weight of you just right in my arms presses out all distractions
from this simple moment
and I am flattened into calm.
I take a breath, my mouth forms the first sound of Amazing Grace
but all that is released is a sigh.
And another.
Again.
Every time it is the same, as if once in my lungs,
the air changes its mind.
My sweet love, I finally accept this gift of yours.
We rest together, held in your stillness,
connected by this need to be at one
through our deep hymn of silence.
The songs will wait.

A Mommy Poem

There is poetry in here.
It's like the computers are on the 6th floor,
humming, waiting,
and I'm stuck in the elevator
between Housewares and Toys with the toddler
who should be home napping
but instead has her hand down the front of my shirt
demanding nuh-nuhs.

Yes, Virginia, there is a room of one's own
but there are also one's children
and their screams and whining outside the door
which tend to fill one's psyche
with images entirely non-poetic.
Maybe it's time for a revision:
a soundproof room of one's own,
or perhaps, simply,
a nanny of one's own.

Sometimes I think there needs to be a *life* of one's own.
Then immediately I sense the web
on which we all dance, sticky enough to keep us
hanging on together in the truth
that there is no life without each other.

There are those moments—never hours—
when the interior landscape rises to surround me
and the words come fast, no edits, onto paper.
And then the world comes through the front door
carrying her lunchbox and homework.
The world lifts up her dirty hands
reaching for the back of my neck,
and the poems are pinched into spaghetti sauce
on the stove. The poems go down the drain
with the dishwater.

11

For Awhile, After You Were Born

How strange now, that I'd thought it would include me:
the bursting forth after waiting,
the coming forward into light, whole.
Every cell remarkable,
the movement like a wave but with no ebb,
unceasing.
Such a sudden, empty stretch of time
once I knew that, sometimes,
I have to be the shell
cast off, broken.

In Bed With The Baby

Shortly after lunch time
I took my clothes back off and got in bed
with the baby.
I had not had them on very long anyway,
about as long as her very short nap
and this way I thought maybe we
could both relax.
She nursed on the left side
then she nursed on the right side
then she sucked on my chin
while I tickled her thighs.
Then for a while she rested her face on my cheek
and said "Uhhhh."
I laid there trying to imagine
the rest of the world with its clothes on,
busy at work,
but then she said "ba ba" in my ear
and sat up to smile
and I forgot.

The One Thing

Something wanting to come out, to be poemed.
It nags and lurks and itches and fits too tight, rubs too loose.
Impatience, incubation a command that no whining
or begging or forcing can change.
Losing myself in novels, I write fragments in my head,
characterizations of people who refuse to settle into place, context.

So much weight. The disintegration of the world envelops me.
Greed. Violence. Greed and violence.
Caught between the need to fly and the need for ground,
my wings beat out of rhythm and my feet slip.
There are too many threads for ten fingers to hold and braid,
hold and braid,
pieces keep dropping, instead of a weave they tangle,
labyrinth into maze.
My mind and heart leap ahead to solutions
but the ways to get us all there are blank spaces on the map.
My body cries *Do Something*.
My brain is soggy with weeping.

Calm and stillness bring sleep, interrupted a thousand times by a
small child's need for comfort in the dark.
That is the one thing I can give.
Sacrifice and blessing, the simple gift of my hand on her cheek,
her body against mine, safety in the surrounding night.

Crave Sleep, Wipe Baby Poop (after *Chop Wood, Carry Water*): A Journal Entry

...but right now, right now I must wait until the baby sleeps, wait until the errands are run. Wait. Wait. And waiting I am hourglass, sieve, though I want to be kettle, cup. Sometimes the great desire to BE demands the courage to be....nothing.

"So are you doing anything besides------------?"

The look at the unfinished end
is always the same:
raised eyebrows, expectancy,
silence where "taking care of a baby" goes.

Anything besides:
Laundry twice a day (at least),
grocery shopping, cooking,
vacuuming so she doesn't put splinters and dust in her mouth,
drinking coffee to stay awake,
changing diapers,
changing diapers clothes shirts socks pants she is almost walking
watching following all senses on alert to potential danger....

This is only the baby stuff.
The nine year-old requires her own attentions.
As does the mate. The cat.
The tired woman in the mirror.

Anything besides?

The lists in my head of things to attend to
have multiplied geometrically
so even the thin winter light coming through my streaked morning
windows is infused with demands.
Then there are those things I desperately hope not to forget—
to abbreviate, to file or pile as I can

so when the time comes I can write, speak, create again.

While the baby naps in brief moments of prone solitude,
I write my already fading revelations.
Setting the words aside
to lift a smiling girl from her crib
can weave a sad braid of conflict:
Joy just to see her,
                despair to drop the pen again,
                and guilt for the tears I have no energy to hide.

Anything besides?
Oh she is worth it,
worth a thousand times the small daily sacrifice of self
that by its nature seems monumental.
She is worth whole universes more than anything
I could "do besides."
From some calm, accepting place inside
where the Mother guides my heart
comes the certainty that "doing" is,
after all,
a concept belonging to another time,
another world
where doing anything attempts to cover the loss
of that which has been granted to me:
the rhythm of love and discovery between souls.

The Next True Story Of My Life

Period Piece

I began to bleed when I was eleven.
Waiting at the toaster I felt something wet
and in the bathroom I found the new stain on
my underpants, like an inkblot: interpret
this. I called to my mother who'd discreetly
left booklets on my desk that summer about
this very thing. I'd studied them intently,
memorizing all the new words: ovary,

fallopian tube, uterus, vagina,
menstruation, trying to understand how they
all connected as if I would be tested.
So I knew the names but I was unprepared
for bloody underwear at breakfast. I was
still unsure if I would see a tiny egg
come out of me or not. My mother said, "You're
shaking like a leaf," and I wanted to cry.

There were pads and belts at first which I hated
when they rubbed and leaked and never stayed in place.
(I'd seen the ads for "sanitary napkins"
in women's magazines when I was little
and thought they were for elegant dinners and
fastidious guests... people who expected
absolute cleanliness.) At school I was sure
people would know and be embarrassed for me.

But secretly I liked it, I liked the smell
of salty earth between my legs and the way
the blood changed from pink to red to black. I thought
my hands began to look more like my mother's
hands and I finally found myself talking
with my friends about it all, even though the
booklets said not to ever mention it to
others. That is when I became a woman:

breaking old ground and scorning taboos against
putting the body into words, shaping my
tongue to fit the sound of admiration and
praise. Twenty-five years later my own daughter
knows that here is not a bloody wound but life
itself immaculate as flesh; on the day
her flow begins we will go outside and dance,
eat cake with red frosting, celebrate it right.

Greeting The River

Here is how I pray today:
I squat down on the sand
and make my hands into a cup, holding them
in the clear shallow sweet smelling river.
To the water swimming into my hands
I say "Hello mountain."
To the water swimming out of my hands
I say "Hello ocean."
To the water always in my hands
I say "Hello now.
Hello now.
Hello."

Bones In This Bed

Have it be the day your period starts, pretty much on time
but almost late.
You are in between; after relief and before cramps.
You feel restless,
so you have the older child watch the younger one
while you go out to finish clearing the buttercups and quack grass
and weeds you've never seen before
from one of the abandoned flower beds inherited with the house
you moved into six months ago.
The sun goes behind clouds.
You keep pulling, shunning the trowel
and digging in so your fingers
hook below the soil to ease up the plant leaving no roots behind.
You mutter, still restless.
The pile of dead weeds comes up to your knees but you still
feel dissatisfied.
You wonder again if maybe dissatisfaction is not something
that ever really goes away.
Like the clouds. Inevitably gathering above you.

There are bones in this bed.
A few here and there at first just under the surface.
In the corner by the big rock you notice the roots of everything
are stronger, holding on to each other.
More bones surface.
You can't tell what kind of animal they belong to.
You wonder if the people who used to live here
just ate a lot of meat
and composted the remains,
or if some pet was buried here.
You wonder what you will find if you really dig deep.
Millipedes and pill bugs appear in dozens, disturbed
and running for cover.
For the first time you actually understand why

medieval philosophers looked at the earth
and saw death instead of life,
a grim darkness, dangerous and female.

You don't stop digging. You pause to swallow
and your throat is dry.
You sense your fingers wanting to recoil;
at the same time you have to stop them from deliberately
clawing deeper into those unseen layers beneath,
this earth so rich and cold.
The clouds press down. The bones rise up.
You watch in your soul your dark bleeding body
lie calmly down to bury herself among worms and roots,
to say to the ground *Me too. Me too.*

Gran

She doesn't quite understand how it all happened
but the years have accumulated,
like the newspapers and empty boxes and all the broken things she
saved because someday someone might want them.
She can't climb the attic stairs anymore,
and the years, full of events remembered, forgotten, and
changed to suit her own story, still add up to ninety.
Even her only son is old, or so he tells her.
She doesn't believe him.

Her husband is ninety-three and needs to die soon.
She won't let him, even though it gets harder and harder to
keep his pills straight, to remember his oxygen schedule.
He still drives, to one store for their meat and bread, another for
her donut holes and lottery tickets.
Last week when he fell and lay on the floor bleeding
from the mouth
she called her son. Then the dentist.
She knows about 911 but hates to call them with their ambulance
because the neighbors might think something is wrong.

She and her husband have always shared the chores; she cooks
and he washes up.
Lately the food is sometimes cold in the middle,
and the scraped remains often miss the garbage pail.
At night the mice hurry about,
their little cheeks stuffed with treats.

The grandchildren write and send pictures,
come to visit in the summer.
They often arrive together, filling their childhood home,
and late at night after their own children are asleep
they drink beer and coffee and talk about the generations.
They can never be sure if it's tragedy or comedy.
They each have their own years of memories,

and realize their love for their grandmother is easier at a distance.
She always greets them with: *When do you have to leave?*
and whatever their answer her response is the same:
Why do you have to leave so soon?
She gives them old ceiling lamps, dusty flour canisters, unfinished
skirts and jackets she'd been making when her eyes went bad.
She gives their children chocolate covered raisins, white gloves
and plastic rain hats,
1950s books on sewing and past issues of science magazines.
They used to take everything out of politeness,
and head straight to Goodwill or the recycling center.
Now they take her offerings
because they know with their acceptance she is
assured of their love.

She doesn't like to feel so bored.
Her day is scheduled around mealtime, naps, pills,
Lawrence Welk, and the News.
There are no milestones left to anticipate.
She surpassed the age of her own mother's death years ago.
Sixtieth wedding anniversary–done.
Grandkids all graduated and married.
Great-grandchildren produced and growing up.
She just might make it to the new millennium but she refuses
to think of the winters waiting between then and now.
Instead she directs her best faith toward winning the lottery.

She doesn't like to feel so lonely.
She sometimes wishes they'd gone ahead and sold their big house
to move to that fancy retirement home several years ago.
Everyone else talked about how good it would be,
but her husband did not want to go live
with a bunch of old people,
and she convinced herself the change would kill him.

She doesn't want him to die and leave her alone.
She doesn't want her son to not be home when she calls.

She doesn't want her grandchildren to forget about her.
She doesn't want to be old and stuck the way she is.
She doesn't want there to be no more options
and she doesn't want to make another decision.
She is tired tired tired and all the years keep
falling from her hold but she is afraid to let go.
She is afraid to lose control,
afraid to go to sleep at night,
afraid of what is coming, of what she knows
will happen next.

Home

The big dipper angled above my house is so familiar,
like a dream that comes every night before sleep.
The repetitive chant of the frog and its mate
comes through the wood like a twilight habit.
The cottonwoods inhale and whisper to themselves,
careful not to wake the sky.

This circle of night, endless and damp with dew,
all the edges smooth so one thing becomes the other.

This is what the mystery has to say.
This is when I know I'm home.

This Poem Will Not Bring Him Back

1.
We arrive together in my dad's small home town,
early autumn California,
cancer in the backseat.
I am eager to see
the stories I grew up hearing.
I know the Chinese temple by the river
is the mysterious and taboo joss house;
the sheet glass windows of an antique store on Montgomery Street
frame the legend of Bopo's cobbler shop:
"Fine Boots and Shoes for Gentlemen and Ladies Made Here."

2.
We stop first along the river where the new park is finished.
There used to be boulders here, all along the banks, Dad says.
We'd jump in, way up by the bridge and come down about here.
Bedrock, we called it, this part of the river;
they'd mined it out and the rocks were everywhere.
I take his picture standing by a tree.

3.
At his grandma's house on Lincoln Street, he says,
I could watch people come to the courthouse water pump,
right across the road.
It was three blocks from my granddad's shoe store,
one block up to Aunt Til's,
two over to Ren and Myra's hardware store.
We see what the architects have done 70 years later
to turn his grandmother's house into law offices.
Godammit, he says. *Hell's bells.*
I go in, up to the second floor and find the back staircase,
the one the boarders used, the one he liked to scoot down
in the dark. It is untouched by change,
still steep and narrow.

4.

My friend Pete worked at his dad's stationery store
two doors down from Bopo's.
Some afternoons we'd sneak out the back alley
and run to the pool hall for a quick game.
"So how old were you then?" I ask, as we walk through the same
alley, see the boarded up doors in the brick wall of the past.
"Oh, probably about twelve."
Around in front, he tries to place where the old Hotel stood
across Montgomery before the fire,
but can't summon the sight.
Jesus Christ, he says. *Damn it to hell.*

5.

We find his mom's first house, between town and Chinatown,
two carpenters working on the new front porch.
Up the back is Cassagrande's, his best friend's house,
still standing across the empty lot.
We'd throw rocks, he says, *to see if we could hit each other.*
One or the other of us would stand out in our yards and shout
Come on! or Are you home? at the top of our lungs
when we wanted to play.
Well hell, he sighs. *Damn it anyway.*

We stand alone together between the worlds.
He doesn't see the boy he used to be
jumping from the banks of the Feather River
into the same clear water that surrendered the trout
cool into the hands of the last living Yahi.

That boy rode out of town on a train to college
then across the country to war.
That boy turned into the man who drove west again
in a new Crosley with a bride and a baby in his eyes.

But I see that boy rise to the surface after plunging

from hot to cold,
shake his wet dark streak of hair into a shower of reflected sun,
scan the riverbank and wonder
what he just heard.
It sounded like his name, or some strange whispered thought
of himself...
Nobody there but the trees.
His friends already gone downstream,
he lets his legs rise into the current.
Feet forward, face to the ageless sky,
he floats forever laughing in his growing bones
to Bedrock.

Instructions On Arrival

At the end of your journey
when you get to the sea,
leave your belongings on a long gray log.
Walk through the dry grass
onto the sand.
Take off your shoes and
whatever the tide go barefoot to the edge where
the water comes in.
While you stand there with your feet going numb
and the salt filming your skin,
close your eyes and with all your heart
whisper the names of those you love
into the rhythm and noise of the surf.

Then be quiet and listen for whatever
comes next.

When You Were My Brother

You were always the oldest.
You were in charge of me
and sometimes bossy about the rules.

You built a ferris wheel with your erector set
and let my pinecone doll ride in it.

When you were my brother
you got a concussion on the slip 'n slide.
You liked the song about purple people eaters.
You pulled my two front teeth out
when they were not quite loose enough
but almost, anyway.

When you were my brother
you played the piano better than anyone else.
You had the *big* bike.
Your favorite was strawberry.
You were really, really smart.

When you were my brother
you liked science fiction and Tom Swift
and books with weird spaceships on the covers.
You went to camp, Spirit Lake, and Jamboree.
You were first bounce or fly, and the pogo stick.
You had beautiful hands.

When you were my brother
you taught me guitar chords and then
gave me your guitar.
You picked beans every summer.
When I crashed my bike and ripped up my knees
you knocked on the bathroom door even
though I didn't want anyone to come in,
and you were the one that picked the gravel

out of my skin and cleaned off the blood.

When you were my brother
you were logical.
You had an infection in your toenail and
came home from the doctor with your whole foot
wrapped up big as a pillow.
You sang harmony.
You did cannonballs off the diving board.

When you were my brother
you were part of a set of two big brothers.
You had your blankie just like I had mine.
You played stand-up bass fiddle and the tuba.

When you left for college I cried and
it was the end of life in our family
as I knew it.
You called me Sis.
I wrote you letters and you wrote back.
Your handwriting was so friendly and clear.

Oh! And when you were my brother
there was that time with the bow and arrow
and the painting in the den
and who was to blame and who would get in
the most trouble.

When you were my brother
you liked golf. Not just playing it
but watching it on TV in the den with Dad.
   BO-RING.
You had adventures and sorrows and successes
I knew nothing about.
I sometimes felt like I didn't know you.

When you were my brother
you could stay so calm.
You got married to someone I didn't know before.
You built a car.
You did computers before they were
even, really, "computers."
You had a laugh that was part surprise
and part appreciation.

When you were my brother
I sometimes wondered why you were
the separate one. And when that happened.
Once when everyone was together at the house
we went for our own walk around the block
and I felt so special, and so loved.

When you were my brother
you loved being a dad, and an uncle.
When you got sick so many years ago from now,
a shield of silence went up around you
and nobody knew the rules.
I don't know where you went–so I was sad and confused
and sometimes angry —
but I'm glad that shield was there for you
when you needed it.

When you were my brother
and we found out you voted for Bush and all that,
I knew that was the only sign I might
ever get that your beautiful brain
really was affected by early-onset Alzheimer's.

When you were my brother
you were always protecting somebody;
sometimes it worked and sometimes it didn't
and now I can't ask you which was which.

34

When you were my brother
we shared the same womb six years apart
with a brother in between and a sister later,
so in a remarkably profound and simple
reality of genetics,
we were never really separate.

The last time I saw you, by yourself,
we were still just us
and I held your hand like we were going to
cross a busy street and you were the big brother
going first to stop the cars.

We knew we would all be OK.
I wanted to be with you and
sing for you as you died but
instead I held you in my heart,
and remembered with a huge smile the last
time you called me Sweetpea,
so in the end there was love
and light, and you are still my brother.

A Figure In The Photograph

When I look through certain scrapbooks
I sometimes see a figure in the photographs
with smooth skin around sad eyes that laugh
and a deep smile.
She is young,
and seems already in the next moment when the shutter blinks.
Thick tangles of hair in braids,
in bandanas, the wind,
or sleep.
She is fluid at the edges even when still.

I look and look for a sign,
a conjunction of background and body,
of body and smile,
any clue in her face
to tell me
what she knew for certain,
what she knew not to forget
when she was me.

On The Rescue Squad
for Kodi Aubert

You try to understand
why you were the one there that day,
why the car could not have stopped a foot, an inch,
a second sooner,
why that toddler was the one to know the sky was falling.

You filled his lungs with your breath.
He filled your mind with his dying.
You wish it had never happened but sometimes
you feel yourself reaching for that place again,
as if to go home.
Your throat closes and your chest burns
when you walk through the dark to look into the rooms
of your own sleeping children.
Night after night, day after day
until the distance closes
and your fear slowly melts in the heat of mystery.
The sirens and cries become mute at the scene in your memory
and a small boy's blood sanctifies your entire life.
His spirit lingers over yours, waiting to be sure
you understand:
pain was a door you opened together,
angels take turns wearing flesh
and nothing dies
nothing dies
nothing
dies.

Marriage, Sometimes

Come up to the surface! you shout, thinking I resist
not from need but out of vanity, stubbornness,
the desire to stay out of reach.
You have little trust in this deep world,
this landscape of inverted mountains
and swirling tides that neither ebb nor flow.
You want to walk
always with your head above your heart,
feet visible beneath.
You can't do that here, and you are
afraid of drowning.

When We Fight

We chew our words and spit them out
like gristle.

We scream like steam whistles are lodged
in our throats.

We fall to our knees as if we'd been
gut shot.

We say *you*. And *always*.
And *I can't*.

We are two bulls locking horns
in the china shop of love.
And in all the broken pieces
it is we who bleed.

Lament Of The Fisherman's Wife

It doesn't matter if I scream like a thousand blue jays
or sit in utter silence until every cell echoes your name
your name.
Nor if I spell it out in dead trees at the shoreline
so the water knows, and the sky.
Nor if I tighten my spine and my breath, my heart,
or loosen myself into sharp rolling tears.
You will not come back until the sea lets you go
unswallowed.

Marriage, Still

Heartbreaking struggle and breathtaking beauty.
Roses and aphids, smooth wood and bent nails.
We are hard work, you and I.
Building the present out of separate pasts,
redefining things we thought we knew the meaning of,
creating a language that includes despair and hope.

Sometimes I wake, my eyes
staring at a garden through glass
and I feel the old familiar aloneness of
not knowing,
of not being where I am.
The words would say   *I want to go home*
and my deepest brain scans the landscape for where
that might be.
There is panic, and sadness, and then the sound of
your hammer rings through the woods,
or your footsteps crunch the gravel,
or your voice drifts through the walls
and I breathe again.
You are the hearth fire,
the open door.
You are the angel hiding in my dreams,
and I am on the path of my life
always coming home
to you.

Mid-Life Crisis

The day one daughter begins to drive, and the other prepares
for second grade,
I look in the mirror and wonder whose body this is.
When did I quit looking like myself and start
looking so much like my mother?
This is a sudden transition,
with sudden hot flashes, sudden
tight waistbands, sudden gray hairs, things just suddenly giving in
to gravity,
and the sudden realization that I am the one living my life
and nobody else can do it, define it, change it or judge it but me.
At just this moment I understand antidepressants
will never be enough,
so I imagine living on a Greek island
in a sun drenched whitewashed villa on a cliff overlooking the
deep blue
Mediterranean.
Yet I know nothing–not pills, placebos, or Paleohora—
will help me escape this bizarre transition into *Phase: Mid-Life.*

How can this be? How can I be in mid-life when I haven't even
quite got the part of being grown up yet?
I thought I'd be an adult by now but I still don't get a lot of
the lingo, like: "financial planning."
I mean, to me that's making sure
there are checks in the checkbook before I hit the grocery store.
I have been able to pass as a grown-up in certain circumstances,
depending on how old everybody else is.
How long they need me to be serious.
If I have to cook or not.
How can this be middle age if I don't have any of the right clothes?

Transition during the births of my children seemed never to arrive,
and then when it did it sucked out everything like a tidal wave
except the deep throbbing notion that I had to survive,

I had to surf the tsunami one wave at a time.
Trapped in my body I pushed,
held, pushed, held like a great artery,
a Mother Heart.

There are no obvious midwives this time, no preparation,
and few accounts yet from other women that come close
to describing this.
But the pulse of identity is so familiar,
the demand for someone's arm to squeeze,
the feeling again that if I ride
the emotional,
hormonal,
seasonal,
cyclical waves of my own body I will survive.
I will come to on another shore where elastic waistbands
are lurid with sexuality,
where the path is clear and not too steep,
where I am a woman living the next true story of my life.

Salmon Dance

I danced with my death last night,
a little flake of salmon
that got lost on its journey while I gasped
in laughter at my friend's story.
Pretty soon I was not choking exactly,
but not breathing well either.
And then I couldn't get a breath in.
Or out.
Everything was full with nowhere to go
and the air was a solid wall with only
my family's faces in movement around me,
my husband's eyes rising and coming nearer.

Much, much later, days after the Heimlich maneuver
restored the flow of oxygen for me,
I recognize another story being enacted that evening:
the earlier death of the salmon we had all
been gratefully, wondrously feasting on.
I was chosen as if by chance to dance the salmon's death
without gills,
raised not from an unwilling sea
but onto my own two feet.
If the salmon had arms it would have
waved them like mine.
If I'd had a tail it would have been trying
to flip its body back into water,
into darkness,
into life.

Heads Up

Don't lean forward on your walks,
the chiropractor warned.
It's too much strain on your back.
Keep your neck in line with your spine,
my yoga teacher says.

But our language tells us
Go ahead
Get ahead
Go head first
Make headway
Fall headlong
Head for the hills.

Our poor heads.
Wanting to be the sweet flower on a stalk,
not some magnetic bowling ball on a stick,
always pulling,
well,
ahead of itself.

Invaders

I. Buttercups

They think I'm approaching them as a postulant: on my knees,
in awe of their power.
Like all gods they have anticipated the blade; it's part of their
cosmology, it's what they tell their little baby buttercups,
the butterthimbles, at bedtime:
"You see, first, children, they bow to our glory, then they worship
with a deep assault, trying to uncover and bring to light the source
of our being. There have been sacrifices, of course, as must be
with their kind, but we reign forever clenched as one, and they fall
to weeping and speaking in tongues.
Sleep well darlings, tomorrow's sun is coming."

II. Slugs

I have resorted to bisecting slugs with my trowel as I clear a way
for the asparagus shoots in the midst of damp weeds.
I used to pick them up and toss them—
into the grass, the gravel, the woods—
until today when I heard a little voice say "Pick *me*, pick *me*!"
and I understood I have been their circus ride,
their metamorphosis; I was giving them wings.
"Wheee!" they would say as they flew through the air,
suddenly weightless.
Then after landing, "Let's do it again!" and the slow but steady
slime back again to the garden.
Well, I thought grimly, as I laid the eager oozing creature
before the blade.
The first ride's free. Then you pay.

Poetic License

As I Lay Dying, Beloved,
a Light in the Attic of the House of Spirits
brings a Separate Peace to the Bluest Eye.

But That Was Then, This is Now,
And The Sun Also Rises, like Clockwork Orange,
like the Heart of Darkness, like the Color Purple.

Sons & Lovers, & Women In Love
Go Tell It On the Mountain
while All the Kings Men Go Ask Alice.

The Naked and the Dead Howl in My Diary
about when Carrie Flew Over the Cuckoo's Nest.

Huckleberry Finn, the Arizona Kid, Ulysses & Harry Potter—
All Earth's Children give us Goosebumps.
But Christine and Captain Underpants Jump Ship to Freedom.

What My Mother Doesn't Know, I Know
Why The Caged Bird Sings In the Night Kitchen:
It's Perfectly Normal.
Metamorphosis.

She Used To Like Winter

Some nights she can quit thinking the sky
is flat, its bright, hidden wounds
unable to bleed.
Instead the sky lies open
and the stars are fingertips
or alphabets
or eyes.
In days without sun the ceiling
slides back into place,
gray as old soup
or the wet ashes of dreams.

She used to like winter especially
near the sea,
when the dark mind of the waves pulled
at her own,
where she slept to the sound of water
swallowing itself.
But now she rakes cold fingers through the earth
for a hungry sight of green shoots
and buys imported mangoes,
those ripening globes of comfort to ponder
in the sleepless dark.
She stares out her blank window into night
and sees the giraffe:
her neck unfolds and disappears
through clouds.

On Mother's Day

She sank deeper and deeper all day,
resting at last.
No listening, no thinking.
The fear that once overwhelmed
all but her breath, forgotten.
As evening came promising the night, she died
so imperceptibly at first it took her by surprise.
Then delight.

One hundred twenty miles to the north
I spent the day on my knees,
sun and clouds at my back as I dug,
tugged and turned my way
around weed-blooming flower beds.
The horizon inches from my nose,
my hands caked brown, pungent lemon balm
and buttercup in my pores.

The call came late, well into the promised night.
When I went to bed later still, I closed my eyes
and saw roots unclenching the darkness,
a hand, and the swift rising lift into the light.

Reflections After Watching a Star-of-Bethlehem Flower
For Twenty Minutes and Feeling Like I'd Been The One
Being Watched, Unfolding

Sometimes I think if we really used our senses,
that all the roads and all the
libraries, offices, the schools, stores, & sidewalks
would just become this huge forest of people
standing struck dumb in awe,
caught in the moment (the sound, the light),
mouths hanging open,
eyes wet with wonder.

If we start today, here,
without the paralysis of linear thought
and just *feel* what our senses bring us,
see how each gift is a whole universe in itself,
is enough for a complete life,
is shaped so the next gift fits into it,
and the next into that,
with enough room still to cradle us as we fall into
the grace of connection—
well, we'll either be lunatics
or mystics
or babies
or clowns,
or maybe we'll just walk one step at a time,
the empty bowls in our tender hands
overflowing.

I Don't Know Your Garden

Or what you might have planted this year
if tanks had not destroyed the topsoil.
Or what you might call weeds and remove
if bombs had not been there first.
You might have been there today, like me,
your fingernails filling with dirt,
your senses with wealth
as you greet the rising perennials, plant bulbs,
converse with a middle eastern cousin of the buttercup.
Are there weeds near the Euphrates, in the Garden of Eden?

I'm digging in my garden,
pondering our intimacy.
The tax on my privilege of working here
sends a rain of bombs onto your head,
the heads of your children, your flowerbeds.

I have seen the bombs on TV but not the shape
of your hands.
I know the names of your enemies but not those
of your daughters,
not the names of your flowers.

I am on my knees in my garden.
You should be too, digging a trench for peas,
not shoveling dirt into your neighbor's grave.

I am on my knees
reaching through the earth
to ask your forgiveness.

Announcement

Today, taking nothing for granted,
I praise with gratitude this most extravagant gift:
This luxury of listening.

Wind moves a chorus of trees into sound -
the cedar, then the maple, then east to the cottonwoods.
The birds - different families of song and chatter-
finch, chickadee, wren and waxwing.
The chirp and buzz of hummingbird.
The drone of mason bees, diligent and driven toward pollen
& back again to the darkness of their round chambers.
The constant undertone of the river,
like a tiny boat
that drifts forever through my ear canal...

The world is breathing my own breath with me.
I belong here, listening.
Listen!
It is all a love story,
a life story,
each moment a birth
day
present.

The How I Want To Die Contest

3rd Place:
So I'm in bed reading a book,
face to the window of sky.
The book gets too heavy like it does,
and I put it down, just for a minute.
I'm not really sleepy yet.
My hand strokes the cat at my side.

2nd Place:
Or maybe I'm outside sitting in the sun.
I turn my face up to the warm birdsong
and summer scent to rest my eyes,
just for a minute.

1st Place and Still In the Distance:
Everyone has gathered—
daughters, husband, best friend, grandchildren.
There are a few tears
as there always must be at the party
where everything matters.
A bon voyage! And it is me who is leaving!
Like a traveler on the deck of a ship:
"Goodbye!" I cry, "Good luck with all that!"
as I watch them standing together,
waving and blowing me kisses.
Then I turn from the rail, already here,
and run toward the music with my dancing shoes on.

July

Oh this sweet familiar only-in-summer view:
the sun turning down toward the hills,
first row of garden blooming through its fence,
cat calm in the green shade watching her dreams,
my knees in the sun.
How was I ever 20, or 30, without this?
And how can I be 60 when this moment—and all things of it—
is timeless and always?
The breeze touches the foxglove,
lifts the dragonfly's path.
The cat turns her head.
Three clouds meet and dissolve in the sky.
I am sinking into the grass, this summer air
my breath.
My body fills with light.

Worship

"I'm really quite happy with my present church," I say, politely.
The small group stands on my porch, pamphlets in hand,
concern in their eyes. I try to imagine what I would say
if asked exactly which church I mean.
In the summer I call it Church of the Holy River.
In winter its name sometimes is
Church of the Blessed Double Windowpane.
Held in the love at Jerry's memorial last month,
we were the Church of Sacred Gratitude for a Friend.
As I put this on paper, I look up to see
the Church of the Divine Maple Who Turns Green into Gold.

I don't know if they would understand this.
I could describe honey with a dozen delectable names
but it would be a poor substitute
for dipping a finger to the comb
and dripping onto the tongue sweet essence of bee.

Come with me, I would have to say.
And we would walk through the thick summer light to the river.
Here are the pews, I could tell them, and help them each find
a place on the round smooth rocks.
We would sit together breathing all the words away
and then there would be just listening, in the sun, to the water,
how it takes all the sounds of bird language, tree murmur,
sky yawning, fish laughter,
and sings them in one wet song.

When the service is over, we would end with a prayer.
Eyes closed, heads bowed, each one a vessel filled
only with praise,
  we think *feather*
  whisper *fire*
  say *ocean*
  cry out *earth.*

Haiku

Thirteen At Work Haiku

The Web site you seek
Cannot be located, but
Countless more exist.

❖

Chaos reigns within.
Reflect, repent, and reboot.
Order shall return.

❖

Program aborting:
Close all that you have worked on.
You ask far too much.

❖

Windows NT crashed.
I am the Blue Screen of Death.
No one hears your screams.

❖

Yesterday it worked.
Today it is not working.
Windows is like that.

❖

Your file was so big.
It might be very useful.
But now it is gone.

❖

Stay the patient course.
Of little worth is your ire.
The network is down.

❖

A crash reduces
Your expensive computer
To a simple stone.

❖

Three things are certain:
Death, taxes and lost data.
Guess which has occurred.

❖

You step in the stream,
But the water has moved on.
This page is not here.

❖

Out of memory.
We wish to hold the whole sky,
But we never will.

❖

Having been erased,
The document you're seeking
Must now be retyped.

❖

Serious error.
All shortcuts have disappeared.
Screen. Mind. Both are blank.

Twenty Haiku

Is it plum blossom
or spring snow through the window?
Either way, light falls.

This constant green wet.
I can feel myself growing
bright vermillion gills.

Insomnia laughs.
Play with me, she says aloud,
as if I love her.

❖

Always enough time
whispers gently in ear of
Never enough time.

❖

Compassion. The gift
hard to give, hard to receive
without practicing.

❖

This one simple thing:
When mind is the obstacle
Just take the next breath.

❖

Old woman winter,
I release you with deep thanks
for reminding me.

❖

River beautiful,
Green and cold from the mountain:
This morning you shine.

❖

The stars are quiet.
Great horned owl calls from night tree.
Mice tremble. I wait.

❖

After this Earth Day
I would like a body day,
And a day of sky.

❖

The dew is rising.
Silence settles in the trees
Dark with sleeping birds.

❖

Full moon at low tide.
Rain eclipses a blue sky.
I am salt, water.

❖

Sit facing the sun.
Squint your eyes barely open.
You will see rainbows.

❖

Haiku for Moments Like This:
We thought we would die.
Instead, from our broken hearts
Compassion spilled out.

❖

Bastille Day:
Knitting needle codes.
That high, waiting blade of sky.
No time to eat cake.
(with apologies to Marie Antoinette.)

❖

Thinking about snow
cold moonlight and calling owls
in all that silence.

❖

On way into town
eagle in tree. On way home
moon in the same tree.

❖

Raking frozen leaves.
Might as well try to rake the stars
from a frozen sky.

❖

Ghost clouds in wet trees.
All day they learned rain songs from
Invisible birds.

❖

Coyotes cry out.
Night shivers her dark response.
Moon bows her head, smiles.

❖

Ancestors, listen!
Nine swans flew out of the clouds
When I sang your names.

The World Split Open

Her Voice

The centuries speak to me in a woman's voice.
In a backward spiral she speaks
with changes of color, cadence,
season, space,
but always in the same language of silence broken.

She has always been the melody of her time.
Under the noise of law,
of civilizations grinding and blasting upward,
the Source murmurs, rests, in dirge or lullaby
according to the rhythm of her nature.

She can scream from a thousand throats
opening like full moons in broad daylight.
She can chant unceasingly
across a thousand hidden altars.
She is heard in dreams, chance, in each moment
when the sky has not yet fallen.

For me she is one voice become many,
many voices in one,
inside the words of women who have also heard.
I listen to my own heart beating.
I listen to the wind at the door.
She is speaking to me,
has never stopped,
and soon
soon
I shall open my mouth
and sing.

Metamorphosis

The woman will not know what she wants.

She will see the bird and wish to fly.
She will see the water and wish to move across it.
She will see the moon through cedar and wish to be
the creature who thrives in darkness.

The woman will not know what she is.

For the man, she is his promise to himself, revealed.
For the boy, she is the sea from which he landed.
For the friend, she is sister in all things.

Perched on a star when the tides are changing
I would tell the moon to send her a dream with wings,
command the wind to carry the chant of mermaids to her ears.

If I dared the night in foraging I would surely find
the mirror she has lost
and hold it while her eyes reflect the secret she is seeking.

Midnight

Hecate at the crossroads waits for you.
You can see her breath, warm vapor in the night chill.
Against the dark cloak of her body she holds her lamp,
its glow a memory of the place before birth.
Three paths move out from the one that brings you here.
You stand before choice, and not choice.

The night has no moon.
No past, no future to swallow or say,
but breath, pulse, and finally, calm desire.
From the flame a voice calls to its mate
in your heart.
Hecate lifts her lamp.
You turn from its blaze of compassion
to face your path.

Inside your shadow a raven spreads its wings.

The Trees

Cottonwood, dogwood, cedar, fir
maple, sumac, apple, pine,
hemlock, hawthorn, juniper, spruce,
willow, cypress, alder, ash,
chestnut, holly, hazelnut, birch.

In their deep fingers the spin of stone and clay,
the dance of dark water and soil,
the rise and descent of seasons.

These ancient tribes carry all that I knew at birth,
all that I now try to remember.
It is a task substantial as the air they shape in colors.
As weightless as the breath inspired by leaf and lung.

All day they hold the light
in the green of needle and leaf,
in the pitch and peel of bark.

Now it is twilight.
Ringing with a silent song
they gather to their topmost limbs the light
then let it go
to shine as stars, to cover the moon,
to guide each dream to its dreamer.

I watch them darken as if in prayer,
suffused with calm and vision spreading far beyond
the boundaries of night.
They see for me what I cannot imagine.
They keep for me what I cannot contain.

Old Woman

Old Woman is dreaming
while spiders mend and wait,
while moonlight moves from the top of the cedar
to the forest floor.
A faint reflection of stars resting in her hair
and the night curled in her hands,
Old Woman dreams of snow and of snow melting
on her tongue,
of laughter on the riverbank and the smell of the sun.
She dreams her mother's voice.
Old Woman is dreaming of her lovers,
of the white limbs of the cottonwood against the sky.
She dreams across valleys
and over the dark rise of mountains.

She is teacher, poet, healer
singer, storyteller, gift giver.
She is a river of tears.
She is laughter in the belly.
She lights the fire
and she puts the fire out.
She sleeps in the ashes and embers and flames
and rises dream-tempered,
warm to the touch.

Remember This

They are running I can hear them
     running for their lives
from the sword that reaches out to slice their souls
     from their bodies, throats left open gleaming raw
from the weight of earth and stone that lies upon them
     crushing bone and lung
from the fire smoke and heat of hell cursed by
     the greedy crowd
from the lives of saints and sinners and the hoofbeats
     turning south.
They run from God and His new and lusting mouth.

They run through forests of night, over the hills of healing
     where the hyssop grows and the dock
where the Mother and Her child in circles
     wider than moonlight walk
where the dreams have come and the ways to see
     and the songs of self enchantment
where power waits underground and green
     in the horn of the stag and the dance.

They run on feet more used to dancing out a rhythm
     finding pathways in a stream
more used to climbing feeling safe within the darkness
     of the sacred caves
Oh how they danced in the sacred groves
     arms raised and waving for the Wheel
     embracing air and everturning time.

In the light of day they weave and work
     planting and soothing
casting out and calling forth the patterns
     and the passions of their lives.

Remember this they whisper to the newborn babe

this sea this flesh of landing and the veil
Remember this they echo to the dying
    this passing and the drifting in between
the mysteries.

    Remember   and they bless the fire
    Remember   and they kiss the air
    Remember   and they purify the water
    Remember   and they sanctify the stone

And so,
the huntsmen's hooves have turned to drumbeat,
    clinking reins to cymbals singing
and they dance they cry they return unto themselves
    Agonized thirst and cooking flesh
    broken back and splintered hips
    disemboweled and tongueless they shall be
no more
    for they are running, running for our lives
into the trees and over hills of time
    down through all the sloping centuries
they come running now
    to waken in my dreams.

Snow White

I am so tired.
It is hard to describe the heaviness,
the way it pulls me down.
My body moves through time, through this house
as if without me.
I lift dish after dish through water,
smooth rough sheets, thread needles, close drawers.
I bring my hands to my face and cannot feel their touch.
I am sinking beneath the surface of my own skin.

I think it started when I first left her.
My mother.
She surrounded me, demanded things of me
I could not give.
Be this. Be that.
She wanted me to be like her, and to not be like her,
to be who she once was, and who she could never be.
I felt she was killing me.
I had to get out.

Now I know.
She was lonely. She had no one to love but me.
And she was afraid for me, afraid for herself
in a world of stories destined to separate us.
I have learned that loneliness here,
when I look in the mirror and see her looking back.

Once in the middle of the day
I looked up from my spinning to see an old woman at the window.
When I went to her she drew an apple from her basket
and pressed it into my hands.
She did not speak when I raised the fruit and took a bite.
The bitterness of it burnt my lips, my tongue,
sent a shock of grief through my bones
and I fell to the floor, covered in a wave

of dark wings.
And when light came again I was on my stool
before the wheel.
No taste in my mouth.
No bruise to my limbs.
I stared toward the window where no one stood.

I cannot get her out of my mind,
that old one and her terrible gift.
I am afraid.
Something awaits me that must be completed,
once and for all.
I know what it is.
For three nights in a row an owl has come
to watch me in my sleep.
She has sent him: my mother,
my mirror,
the one at the window.
He is watching me now.
When I close my eyes and am perfectly still
I can hear the sound of the sky under his wings.
I can almost feel his breath, like a feather,
on my lips, my neck.
I must lie down, here, near the threshold.
I can no longer move.
I will sink until I can go no deeper.
There is no other way
but down.

The Monster In The Basement

We knew he was bad.
The mean dad in the neighborhood
whose whistle cut through our play, a shrill
somebody's in trouble! —
instead of just the *dinner's ready* signal.
He kept the strap he used on his kids
hanging by his kitchen door with the coats.
He yelled from his driveway and we ran,
scattering like pool balls on the break,
leaving his daughters, our playmates, behind
as we flew down the street toward home.

We rode in back seats with our cats or dogs
when our parents took them to the vet for their shots,
when he was the vet.
We wondered in our backyards how he could be so nice
to animals.
Playing one day at their house I opened the refrigerator
for the lemonade and there was a big eyeball in a jar,
right next to the French dressing.
It's from a cow, his daughter told us.
He's a butcher now.
Our parents didn't seem to know
what we knew.

The mom was like a wilted flower.
She made us go home when we had to pee.
She pulled her daughters' hair into ponytails so tight
their blue eyes looked Asian.
It was on a Sunday night during Walt Disney that she came
running down the street crying and shouting
and some of our dads walked up the sidewalk to her house
while she stayed with the moms who had collected on a porch.
Then she went away to a hospital until school was out
and came back with a weird smile and a laugh

that for some reason was really saying *don't tell*
and I wondered by myself if she was really their mom
or someone else who came back instead.

Something happened to me that goes with his name;
it comes into my head
when my mind lets go of the story and falls like an accident
into the abyss.

I tried to fall all the way down
to where I could finally land and face him,
the monster in the basement,
and though I spent years with the wind in my face
there was no landing.
Instead I learned to catch the updraft
and leave him in the dark
where every now and then he plucks a nerve,
a sound that stings a survival meridian,
catches my day long breath until I can exhale again.
But mostly he is banished.
He is silent.
He is past.

Demeter Speaks To The Terrible Sons
(Upon the abduction and murder of A.S., age 18,
Thanksgiving weekend, 1989)

None of you seem to know who I am.

There is a body in the river
that was meant to cross over.

The stories told of me
hang by strings on this web you call time,
and are heavy with silence.
The soul of this web is a weight,
cast in a darkness not of night
but of loss.

There is a body in the river
that was meant to cross over
and find the truth in shadows.

I am going to cut these strings.
I have done it before, once,
when my voice would not be heard,
when you thought to string me up in death.
You beheld the barrenness
of life without me.
Why was that not enough?

There is a body in the river
that was meant to cross over
and come back
to me.

Instead she lies alone and cold.
And I am dumb in the darkness
with the weight of webs
of words telling stories strung with lies.

When I take this knife and cut
your very bones may snap as well.
May your fields turn to ash.
May your seed turn to stone.
May you be alone with grief to lick the salt
that runs like rivers
across your face.

She Comes To Reason

She always cleaned up afterwards
—the broken chair, the shattered plates—
fixed things up to hide the signs,
wore clothes that covered the bruises.
Made excuses.
She could not clean up the shouts
and cries that broke against the walls and sifted down,
settled into the sofa, the rug,
broke against her body and sifted down
inside.

One night he came home and told her to start cooking,
his friends were coming for dinner.
"How can I fix dinner when there's no food here?" she asked,
knowing it would be her fault,
unable to summon food from thin air
or money from his pockets.
He beat her.
She protected her growing baby belly, took the blows
on her face
until the taste of blood brought her to reason.

She wiped the blood and smeared it on the walls.
Wiped the blood and drew red curving lines on white paint.
Wiped the blood,
wiped the blood and drew herself in the art of naming.

He tried to stop her.
With the wave of an arm she sent him flying
away from her glory.

It was finished when the blood flow ebbed.
She sank down in silence
and watched
while he cleaned it up.

Sister Lost

(Hebrew tradition tells the story of Adam and Lilith, the first man and the first woman created by God in the Garden of Eden. Lilith was a passionate, forthright and independent woman who did not acquiesce to Adam's demands that he be above her, in the sexual act as well as in the more general sense. Acting upon Adam's subsequent complaint, God is said to have banished Lilith from the Garden and created Eve as a more suitable, submissive replacement. At least until the Apple Incident.)

I. Eve Tracking Lilith

There are times I need to go down the path alone,
without him,
without the words of naming falling from his lips
like seeds filling my ears
so that is all I hear.

This is the way:
To wake before his dreams release him,
start down the path in the wet of new morning.
Like a ring of water I widen my circle
each time I wander.

o

I am certain now there is someone else.
Someone whose footprints fit mine
but are not mine.
I know where I have and have not been
and I find the signs of her —
    the smell
    the sound of her —
that linger just inside
each place I did not go before.

Today I shall pass through the stillness,

83

let the shadow of her steps become my own.
My hands are full with the need
to reach across the truth for her.
I want to see her, and I am afraid
of nothing but the silence
where her name belongs.

II. Lilith to Eve

Oh yes my sister, I have watched your wanderings
through this placed called Garden.
I am here, unseen but sensed,
unbounded by shall nots,
and certainly, my dear one, unnamed by him.

I feel your life as you cannot,
the life taken from you with promises of sweet beginnings
and savage threats of suffering.
You are tracking the mirror that knows your own name,
that knows your own body,
a landscape that rolls
rich and fertile down to the sea.

I have seen you, sister,
and have ached for the caution of your heart's pulse
strong enough for life but not for passion.
That heart afraid to bite its fruit of fullness,
afraid his sword will spring forth to destroy.
You have yet to learn that what shall be destroyed
is not yourself but his lies.

I know I must approach you
and I know the way it will be told:
The serpent, the tree and the fruit,
the curses and exile,
as if snake is not sacred
as if tree is not friend

as if apple is not gift
and as if you, my sister,
are not power of birth, death and life everturning
at home anywhere you squat to bleed,
with eyes to see through death's slave dressed as Angel,
with body to ignite his soul in grief for what he has lost,
with voice to name yourself
and hands to fling wide the gate
on your way out.

Gloria Matri (a version of *Gloria Patri*)

Glory be to the Mother
and to the Maiden
and the Holy Crone.
As She was in the Beginning
is now and ever shall be.
Circle of Three.
Blessed be. Blessed be.

Winter Solstice

We lit the candles
on the longest night and did cast the circle
around our hearts.

Calling to the darkness
we raised the wind and in the wind
did come the power.

When I prayed to the Mother
out loud in my voice
She did answer me with the breath
of my sisters.
When my sisters prayed I did answer them
with the voice of She who was there
in the dark.

When I came home She did come home
with me
and now is resting
in the space between the mirror
and my eyes.

I am glad to see Her there where
Her smile catches light.

Women's Lit 301

I. Taking It Personally

So many dead women.
The more I read the more
their bodies fall across the pages
limp as fish,
transparent as empty glass
but solid at the edges.

Edna swims to oblivion, Virginia just wades in
with rocks clenched in her pockets.
Taking dinner from the oven
Sylvia fits her head on the rack.
Anne idles the engine, garage doors down.
Anonymous swallows pills past her silent tongue.

Sure and spinning,
caught on the hooks
they untie their aprons, set down their pens,
give up,
turn their backs,
give in.

II. Talking It Over with Papa

So, Mr. Great Writer, you have not escaped me after all.
Your specter hangs above my head
waving white-sheeted arms like some flailing matador
at this windmill of women's names.
You're not on this syllabus, Papa.
In fact you are perhaps the best
example
of what this is
not about, you
know:

fishing, smoking, fighting
and those short breath sentences of testosterone.
Straight up.

Oh, you're still on other lists, for christsake Ernest,
you're Hemingway.
They aren't going to just throw you out,
no matter how good the women are.

III. The Question

Eulogies resist these figures of flesh and paper,
then rise in grief and bite.
I feel angry and cheated
but can't decide what I think.

Then it dawns on me tonight—
refrigerator door open, lettuce in my hand—
you killed yourself too.
Granted, no gracious walk into water,
no keeping it in the kitchen.
You blew your brains out right by the front door.
You were Ernest Hemingway,

you'd put the balls back in literature,
then just like these women you silenced yourself.

So answer me this when you're done reading
over my shoulder:
Was it courage or surrender,
victory or defeat?

The women are still too deep inside
for me to ask them.

Our Woman Line

Stone wheelers, fate dealers, witches and hags,
Feelers and healers and bitches and nags,
Priestesses, mothers, daughters and crones,
I walk in your footsteps. You live in my bones.

You at your dishwashers, typewriters, tables,
You who read recipes, documents, fables,
You in your living rooms, kitchens and beds,
They move in your bodies. They dream in your heads.

Some lived in castles, some lived in caves.
Some sang on the mountains, some danced in the waves.
Some gave birth to others, some lived all alone
and some died in fire. In us they live on.

Collect Your Thoughts

"Here at this place of torment a group of men
were massacred and burnt by Nazis. Collect your thoughts."
— plaque at Laudy's barn at Oradour sur Glane, France

And here are children starving, again, to death.
Over here, this field? Flesh and bone under soil.
Here is the torture chamber, once a gymnasium
where students played for endurance and strength.
Most grew up to die under bullets and knives;
it is their children whom only hunger loves now.
This is not your hometown,
or even your country.
There are no trees and the uniforms are different.
Still, I hope you begin to understand.

Don't change the channel, put down the newspaper,
turn off the sound.
Here at this place, and here, and here, the world waits for you.
See? Her eyes have nowhere else to look.
It's OK if you stare out the window.
It often takes time to sink in.
You must have courage.
Collect your thoughts.
Rassemblez vos pensées.
Raccogliere i tuoi pensieri.
Sammeln sie ihre gedanken.

Years Later

I tend the campfire, pushing the branches further in,
feel such sudden intensity of heat on my face I have to turn away,
ashes in my hair.
And I see them again, standing at the opened windows,
caught above the 84th floor.
My own mind,
too close to a simple campfire,
gives way to the sense of green rivers, blue depths,
to the simplicity of water.

And now I believe that when we thought they jumped,
they flew instead
into an ecstasy of sky
and without even dying
became angels.
What continued to fall was only what they had already forgotten
of fire.

The Blue Burqas Of Kabul

hang lifeless on racks in clothing shops
and street markets,
backs pressed to fronts in uneven rows of one color.
A moving eye could almost summon
from these walls of stitchery
a wave of the sea.

Out among the living
they are fluttering wings.
They are sails,
graceful blue billows of air.
They hide something.
Hands emerge from these mysteries
to touch the faces of children,
to exchange slips of paper for rice.
There are voices but no throats.
There are latticed windows for eyes.
There is,
somehow,
a woman
moving inside each floating
                              blue
                                  planet.
Invisible.

She carries a weight on her head.
She holds pain behind eyes that cannot see a world
without lines and bars across it.
Only later,
away from sky, earth, tree, bird,
away from men,
will she show herself to herself, to her children,
to the four walls of her room.

There are flocks of blue birds with blinded eyes
filling the streets of Kabul.
They do not sing.
They cannot fly.

Witch Story
Or: When We Were The Witches

There are times the witches will not let me sleep.
I sit up in bed, giving in,
and behind my eyes the darkness changes.
I see their faces, waiting.
They do not nag.
Five hundred years of silence has brought them great patience.
It is I who itch with impatience, feel compelled to search
my vocabulary,
fill pages with a list of words that mean *fire*.

From ink-faded paper and computer screens
I learn who they are:
The herbalist and midwife.
The crone and the maid.
The widow with children.
Or property.

I meet them in my imagination:
Old, young, comely or crooked,
headstrong, or hearty,
or hurt.
I hear their chants of worship
in temple, cathedral, forest, mosque.
Some are always silent. Some will speak out.
And some do not suffer fools.

Isabelle has a raucous laugh,
Claire is always in tears.
Anna can read. Elspeth is blind.
Gemma has doubts. Helga has faith.
Every one of them a female body.

Dark ages ago,
the Goddess was buried under earthquakes of invasion

and war.
Now, the winners begin to burn their own mothers,
their daughters,
those others.
The women of Europe, unwilling torches lighting the way
through the Renaissance.

This is my heritage.
Can I find a way to tell this story?
Mustn't we all speak for the dead?
Patient eyes look out from our own faces.
The witch heart is beating like a drum
pulsing in my ears.

Let us sit here together
to tell their stories with our own.
Let us reach across time and the flaming tongues of fire.

My Ancestors, My Self

I do not have curves without gravity.
My ears no longer hold up my jaw line.
More flesh covers my bones than when I was twenty,
or forty.
I look at that girl and accept what I didn't know.
So now I say little sisters, see how lovely you are
without trying:
a moment of nature and beauty in agreement.
The visible body belongs to you.
Mine holds stories invisible.

Here is what you won't see:
there are entire villages in my spine,
migrating tribes who spent generations to settle;
every day I carry the children and rivers and dirt floors
and cooking fires
on this bridge between earth and sky.

My pelvic bones feel the magnetic pull of mountains.
When I lie down at night the forests move,
tendons shifting to hold the soil in place.

My arms like water weeds drift in curving dark currents
and hold time, hold tears, hold tight.

The front of my heart is the sunrise,
the back of my heart the sunset.
I have lived worlds and still I rise each morning,
invisible woman, worlds indivisible, alive
with each breath I take.

On Lummi Island

Everyone up early with the baby.
A little coffee, some fruit salad and leftover pie,
enough for the clouds to pass over the cove
and the sun to return sparkling on the riptide.

Now everyone is back to sleep—
on a bed, the window bench,
in a hammock swinging lullaby,

and it's me and the purple martins
out singing in the southerly breeze
that ripples up wrinkles so the surface of the bay
is a watery brain of no words,
no tides,
just sound and salt

and all that light.

Gratitudes to:

My beloved family, near and far, here and gone, and all honorary members of the Holub Clan; my dearest circle sisters; the library ladies; Bellingham Threshold Singers; and the poets whose work & stories inspire & challenge me.

To Osa and Jamaica, because unconditional love, and to Alan, because everything.

And to poet and friend Don Mitchell, whose generosity of spirit, time, and skill blessed this book into existence.

You must have a song
Waiting, silent in the dark.
Find it by singing.